PIANO • VOCAL • GUITAR

winter won[d]er[lan]d
& OTHER CHRISTMAS [F]AV[O]RI[T]ES

ISBN 978-1-4768-1262-5

HAL•LEONARD®
CORPORATION
7777 W. BLUEMOUND RD. P.O. BOX 13819 MILWAUKEE, WI 53213

Visit Hal Leonard Online at
www.halleonard.com

ALL I WANT FOR CHRISTMAS IS MY TWO FRONT TEETH

Words and Music by
DON GARDNER

BLUE CHRISTMAS

Words and Music by BILLY HAYES
and JAY JOHNSON

I'll have a blue Christ-mas, with-out you. _____ I'll be so

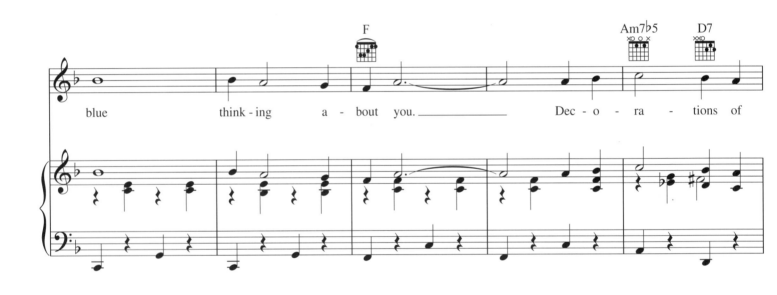

blue think-ing a-bout you. _____ Dec-o-ra-tions of

red on a green Christ-mas tree won't mean a thing if

BRAZILIAN SLEIGH BELLS

By PERCY FAITH

Bright Samba

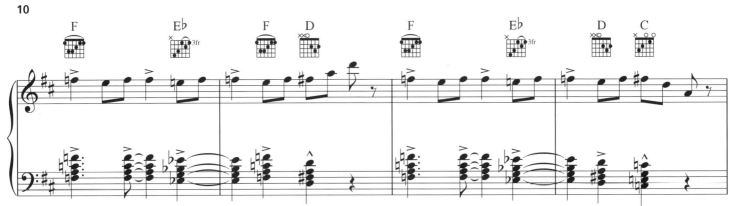

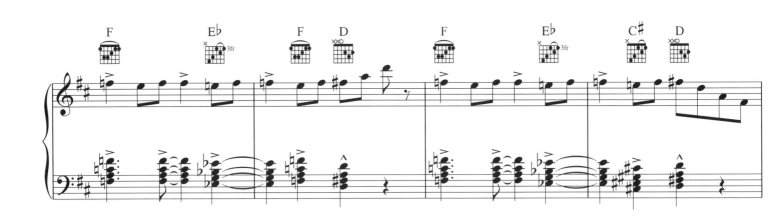

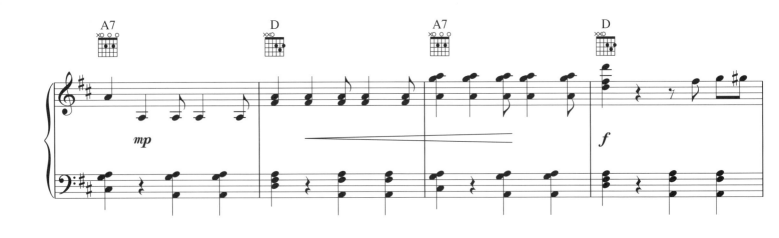

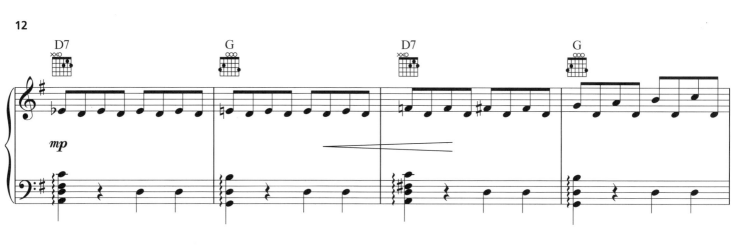

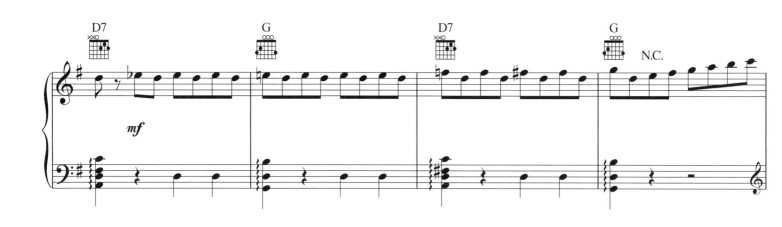

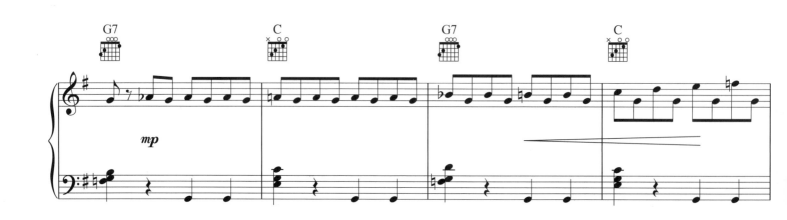

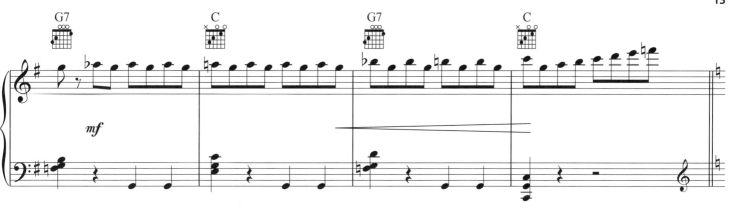

A CHILD IS BORN

Music by THAD JONES
Lyrics by ALEX WILDER

CHRISTMAS AULD LANG SYNE

Words and Music by MANN CURTIS
and FRANK MILITARY

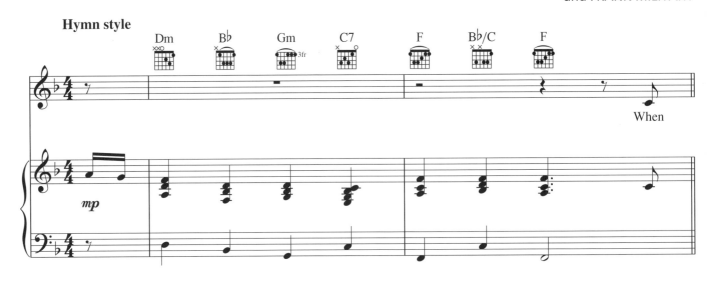

mis - tle - toe and tin - sel glow, paint a yule - tide val - en -
sleigh bells ring and choirs_____ sing and the chil - dren's fac - es

tine. Back home I go to those I know_____ for a
shine, with each new toy we share their joy_____ with a

CHRISTMAS IN KILLARNEY

Words and Music by JOHN REDMOND
and FRANK WELDON

CHRISTMAS TIME IS HERE

from A CHARLIE BROWN CHRISTMAS

Words by LEE MENDELSON
Music by VINCE GUARALDI

THE CHRISTMAS WALTZ

Words by SAMMY CAHN
Music by JULE STYNE

DO THEY KNOW IT'S CHRISTMAS?
(Feed The World)

Words and Music by BOB GELDOF
and MIDGE URE

Medium Rock

It's Christ-mas-time, there's no need to be a-fraid. _

At Christ-mas-time, we let in light _ and we ban-ish shade. __

And in our world _ of plen-ty _____ we can spread a smile _ of joy. _

GROWN-UP CHRISTMAS LIST

Words and Music by DAVID FOSTER
and LINDA THOMPSON-JENNER

JINGLE-BELL ROCK

Words and Music by JOE BEAL
and JIM BOOTHE

HARD CANDY CHRISTMAS

from THE BEST LITTLE WHOREHOUSE IN TEXAS

Words and Music by
CAROL HALL

HAVE YOURSELF A MERRY LITTLE CHRISTMAS

from MEET ME IN ST. LOUIS

Words and Music by HUGH MARTIN
and RALPH BLANE

THE LITTLE DRUMMER BOY

Words and Music by HARRY SIMEONE,
HENRY ONORATI and KATHERINE DAVIS

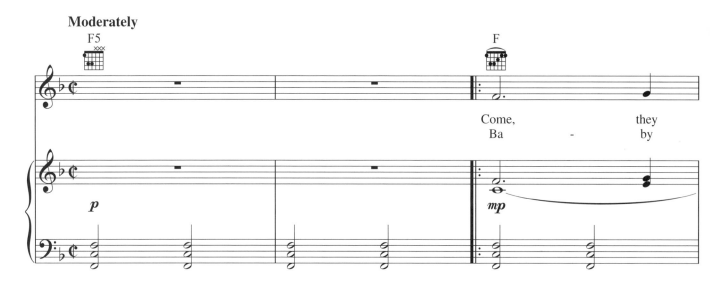

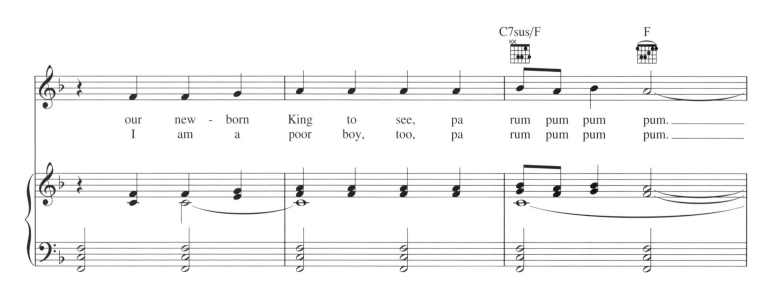

A MARSHMALLOW WORLD

Words by CARL SIGMAN
Music by PETER DE ROSE

LITTLE SAINT NICK

Words and Music by BRIAN WILSON
and MIKE LOVE

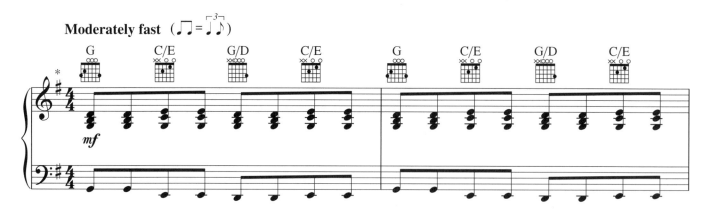

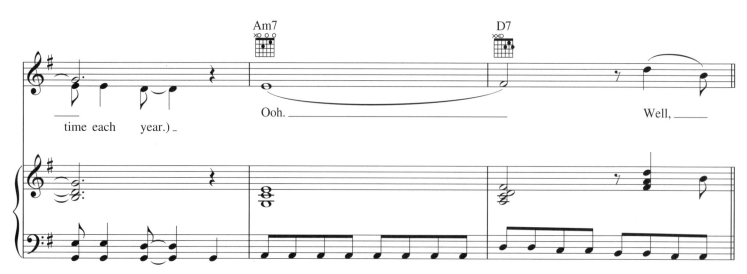

* *Recorded a half step lower.*

way up north where the air gets cold, ___ there's a
lit - tle bob - sled, we call it Old Saint Nick, ___ but she'll
haul - in' through the snow at a fright - 'nin' speed ___ with a

tale a - bout Christ - mas that you've all been told. ___ And a
walk a to - bog - gan with a four - speed stick. ___ She's
half a doz - en deer ___ with ___ Ru - dy to lead. He's

real fa - mous cat all dressed up in red, ___ and he
can - dy ap - ple red with a ski for a wheel, and when
got - ta wear his gog - gles 'cause the snow real - ly flies, and he's

MERRY CHRISTMAS, DARLING

Words and Music by RICHARD CARPENTER
and FRANK POOLER

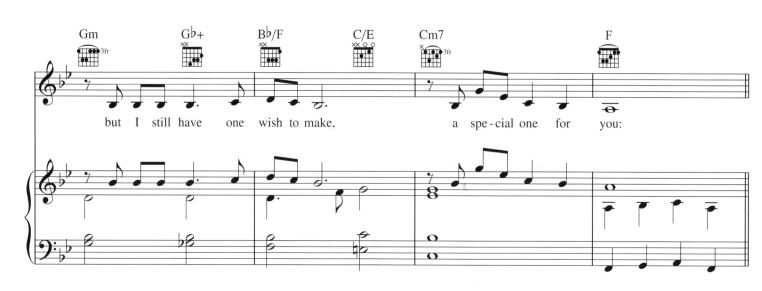

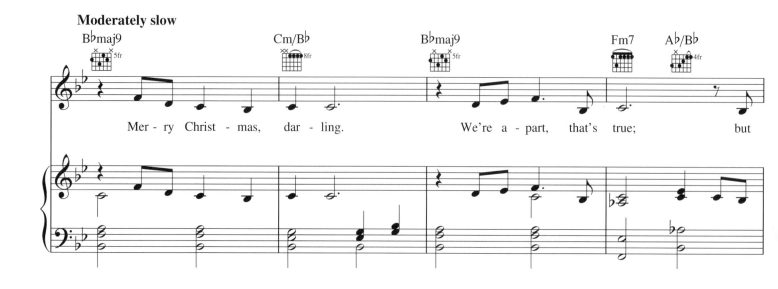

SNOWFALL

Lyrics by RUTH THORNHILL
Music by CLAUDE THORNHILL

Lyrics: Snow - fall, soft - ly, gen - tly drift down.

MISTLETOE AND HOLLY

Words and Music by FRANK SINATRA,
DOK STANFORD and HENRY W. SANICOLA

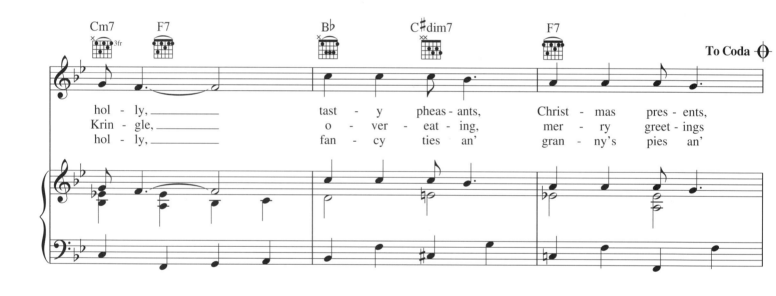

SILVER BELLS

from the Paramount Picture THE LEMON DROP KID

Words and Music by JAY LIVINGSTON
and RAY EVANS

SLEIGH RIDE

Music by LEROY ANDERSON
Words by MITCHELL PARISH

SUZY SNOWFLAKE

Words and Music by SID TEPPER
and ROY BENNETT

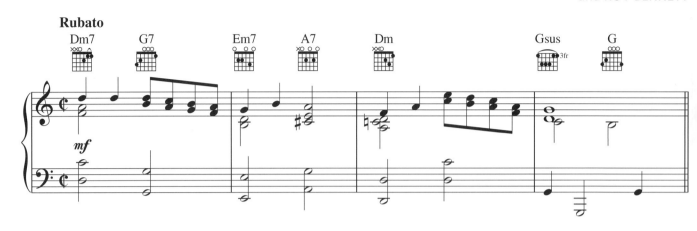

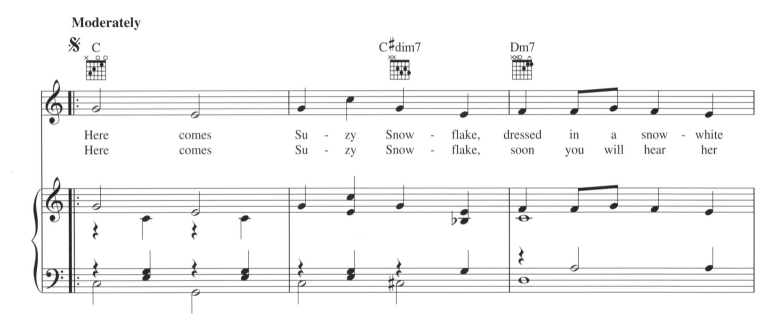

Here comes Su-zy Snow-flake, dressed in a snow-white
Here comes Su-zy Snow-flake, soon you will hear her

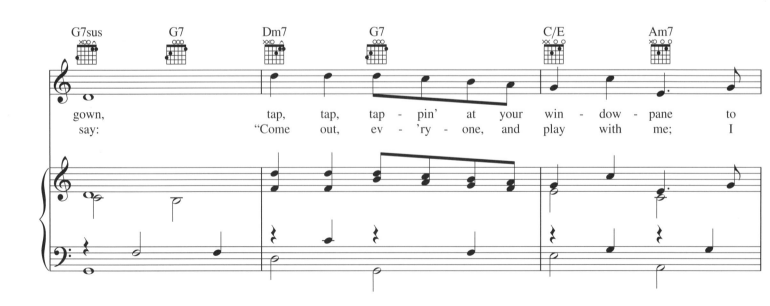

gown,   tap, tap, tap-pin' at your win-dow-pane to
say: "Come out, ev-'ry-one, and play with me; I

WINTER WONDERLAND

Words by DICK SMITH
Music by FELIX BERNARD

WHITE CHRISTMAS

from the Motion Picture Irving Berlin's HOLIDAY INN

Words and Music by
IRVING BERLIN

YOU'RE ALL I WANT FOR CHRISTMAS

Words and Music by GLEN MOORE
and SEGER ELLIS